● soho
● theatre company

Soho Theatre Company presents

MR NOBODY

by **Philip Ralph**

First performed at Soho Theatre on 4 June 2003

Performances in the Lorenz Auditorium

Soho Theatre is supported by

 **Bloomberg**

Registered Charity No: 267234

Soho Theatre Company has the support of the Pearson Playwrights' Scheme sponsored by The Peggy Ramsay Foundation.

MR NOBODY
by **Philip Ralph**

Tommy	Niall Buggy
Jean	Patricia Kerrigan
Claire	Maggie McCarthy

Director	Jonathan Lloyd
Assistant Director	Sarah O'Gorman
Designer	Soutra Gilmour
Lighting Designer	Johanna Town
Sound Designer	Matt McKenzie

Production Manager	Nick Ferguson
Stage Manager	Ros Terry
Deputy Stage Manager	Dani Youngman
Assistant Stage Manager	Vicky Charalambous
Chief Technician	Nick Blount
Chief Electrician	Christopher Wagner
Technician	Ade Peterkin
Scenery built and painted by	Robert Knight
Casting	Ginny Schiller

Advertising: MandH Advertising
Graphic Design: Jane Harper
Photography: Colin Hawkins / Getty Images

Soho Theatre and Writers' Centre
21 Dean Street
London W1D 3NE
Admin: 020 7287 5060
Fax: 020 7287 5061
Box Office: 020 7478 0100
www.sohotheatre.com
email: box@sohotheatre.com

THE COMPANY

Cast

Niall Buggy Tommy

Niall joined the Abbey Theatre at the age of sixteen. His many Abbey credits include *The Cherry Orchard*, *The Seagull* and *Juno and the Paycock*. Other Irish credits include *The Playboy of the Western World* and *London Assurance*. Other theatre credits include *Waiting for Godot*, *The Birthday Party*, *Salad Days* (Crucible Theatre); *No Man's Land* (Gate Theatre); *Hamlet*, *Arms and the Man*, *Travesties* (Haymarket Theatre, Leicester); *Blood Knot*, *Spokesong*, *The Actress and the Bishop* (King's Head, London); *Dwarfs*, *The Shadow of a Gunman* (Young Vic); *The Rivals*, *Love for Love*, *Rough Crossing*, *Threepenny Opera* (Royal National Theatre); *Aristocrats* (Hampstead Theatre – Time Out Award, Clarence Darwent Award, Manhattan Theatre Club, New York Obie Award, Drama Desk Award nomination) and *Give Me Your Answer, Do!* (New York and London). In the West End theatre credits include *Inspector Calls*, *Dead Funny* (Vauderville Theatre – for which Niall won an Olivier Award); *Memoir*, *Spokesong*, *Vanilla* and *Juno and the Paycock* (Best Actor Regional Theatre England Award). With the O'Casey Theatre Company, US and Ireland *The Shadow of a Gunman* (Helen Hayes Award nomination); *Song at Sunset* (one man show New York and London); *Uncle Vanya* (Dublin, New York, Irish Times Best Actor Award); *That Time* (London and also on film). Television credits include *Upwardly Mobile*, *Agony Again*, *Full Wax*, *Father Ted*, *Once in a Lifetime*, *The Gathering Seed*, *Red Roses for Me*, *The Little Mother*, *Chinese Whispers* and *Cruise of the Gods*. Film credits include *A Portrait of the Artist As a Young Man*, *The Lonely Passion of Judith Hearne*, *Close My Eyes*, *The Playboys*, *Kind David*, *Philadelphia*, *Here I Come!* and *Alien 3*.

Patricia Kerrigan Jean

Theatre credits include *Falling*, *Beautiful Thing* (Bush Theatre); *King Lear* (The Globe Theatre); *Memory Of Water*, *Shang A Lang* (National tours); *Abandonment* (Traverse Theatre); *The Storm* (Almeida Theatre); *Macbeth* (Bristol and tour); *Love's Labour's Lost*, *Women Laughing* (Royal Exchange); *The Duchess Of Malfi*, *All's Well That Ends Well* (Royal Shakespeare Company); *Carthaginians* (Hampstead Theatre); *Twelfth Night*, *El Cid* (Cheek By Jowl). Television credits include *Doctors*, *Macbeth*, *A Skirt Through History*, *The Bill*, *A Fatal Inversion*, *Playing for Real*, *Dalziel and Pascoe*, *The Crow Road*, *Flowers of the Forest* (all BBC); *Where the Heart Is* (ITV); *Medics*, *Sherlock Holmes*, *The Magic Toyshop* (Granada); *Dr Finlay's Casebook*, *Taggart* (STV); *Shrinks* (Euston Films) and *Imaginary Friends* (Thames). Film credits include *To Kill a King* (Natural Nylon/Union); *The Find* (Bold Eagle) and *Joyriders* (Joyrider Productions).

Maggie McCarthy Claire

Theatre credits include *Amid the Standing Corn* (Soho Theatre); *Fanshen, The Shaughraun, The Night of the Iguana, Macbeth, Mountain Giants* and *Mother Clap's Molly House* (Royal National Theatre); *The Garden Girls* (The Bush Theatre – Time Out Performance Award Winner); *The Crucible* (Young Vic); *Golden Pathway Annual* (Mayfair); *Byrthrite, The Seagull, Thickness of Skin* (Royal Court); *The Steward Of Christendom* (Out of Joint at the Royal Court, BAM New York, The Gate, Dublin); *Cat with Green Violin* (Orange Tree); *Sailor Beware* (Lyric, Hammersmith); *The Storm* (Almeida); *Drummers* (Out of Joint tour and Ambassadors); *The Merchant of Venice, Rose, Billy Liar* (Belgrade, Coventry); *Clouds* (Nuffield, Southampton); *All's Well That Ends Well* (Birmingham Rep); *Space Invaders, Quartz* (Traverse, Edinburgh); *Travesties, Stirrings in Sheffield, Twelfth Night, Getting On, Slag* (Sheffield Crucible); *Scrape Off The Black* (West Yorkshire Playhouse) and *Misery* (Leicester Haymarket). Television credits include *She's Out, All Quiet on the Preston Front, Hello Girls, Berkeley Square, Trial and Retribution V, Ready When You Are Mr McGill, Death in Holy Orders* and *Servants*. Film credits include *Firelight, Hilary and Jackie, Angela's Ashes, Esther Khan, Ali-G Indahouse* and *Calender Girls*. Radio credits include *The Archers, Citizens* and many plays for Radio 3 and 4.

Company

Soutra Gilmour Designer

Theatre includes: *Antigone* (Citizens Theatre, Glasgow); *Peter Pan* (The Tramway, Glasgow); *The Birthday Party* (Sheffield Crucible); *Fool For Love* (English Touring Theatre); *Macbeth* (English Shakespeare Company); *Hand In Hand* (Hampstead Theatre); *Modern Dance For Beginners* (Soho Theatre); *Tear From A Glass Eye, Les Justes, Ion, Witness* and *The Flu Season* (The Gate Theatre); *Sun Is Shining* (BAC Critic's Choice Season); *The Woman Who Swallowed A Pin, Winters Tale* (Southwark Playhouse); *The Shadow of a Boy* (National Theatre) and *Through The Leaves* (Southwark Playhouse and Duchess Theatre). Opera credits include: *Eight Songs For A Mad King* (World Tour); *El Cimmaron* (Queen Elizabeth Hall, Southbank); *Twice Through The Heart* (Cheltenham Festival); *Bathtime* (ENO, Studio); *A Better Place* (ENO, Colesium).

Jonathan Lloyd Director

Associate Director at Soho Theatre where he has directed *Modern Dance for Beginners, Julie Burchill is Away, School Play, Jump Mr Malinoff Jump, The Backroom* and *Skeleton* and the Under-11s Playwriting Scheme. Other productions include *The Backroom* (Bush); *Perpetua* (Birmingham Rep); *Summer Begins* (RNT Studio / Donmar); Channel Four Sitcom Festival (Riverside Studios); *Serving It Up* (Bush);

Blood Knot (Gate) and *Function of the Orgasm* (Finborough). As a writer for children's television: *Dog and Duck* (ITV) *You Do Too* (Nickelodeon).

Matt McKenzie Sound Designer

Matt McKenzie came to the UK from New Zealand in 1978. He toured with Paines Plough before joining the staff at the Lyric Theatre Hammersmith in 1979 where he designed the sound for several of their productions. Since joining Autograph in 1984, Matt has been responsible for the sound design for the opening season of Soho Theatre; *Vertigo* (Guildford); *Saturday, Sunday, Monday, Easy Virtue* (Chichester); *Frame312* (Donmar); *Iron* (The Traverse and Royal Court). In the West End theatre credits include *Made in Bangkok, The House of Bernarda Alba, A Piece of My Mind, Journey's End, A Madhouse in Goa, Barnaby and the Old Boys, Irma Vep, Gasping, Map of the Heart, Tango Argentino, When She Danced, Misery, Murder Is Easy, The Odd Couple, Pygmalion, Things We Do For Love, Long Day's Journey into Night* and *Macbeth*. For Sir Peter Hall credits include *Lysistrata, The Master Builder, School for Wives, Mind Millie for Me, A Streetcar Named Desire, Three of a Kind, Amedeus* (West End and Broadway). Matt was Sound Supervisor for the Peter Hall Season (Old Vic and The Piccadilly) and designed the sound for *Waste, Cloud 9, The Seagull, The Provok'd Wife, King Lear, The Misanthrope, Major Barbara, Filumena* and *Kafka's Dick*. Work for the RSC includes *Family Reunion, Henry V, The Duchess of Mafli, Hamlet, The Lieutenant of Inishmore, Julius Caesar* and *A Midsummer Night's Dream*. Matt's musical work includes *The Bells Are Ringing, Talk of the Steamie* (Greenwich); *Love off the Shelf* (Nuffield Theatre Southampton); *Forbidden Broadway, Blues in the Night* (West End); Matthew Bourne's *Car Man* (West End and International tour); *Putting It Together* and *The Gondoliers* (Chichester); *Oh What A Lovely War* (Derby Playhouse); the co-sound design at *Tess* (Savoy) and *Alice in Wonderland* (RSC).

Sarah O'Gorman Assistant Director

Sarah is a TV Director, working mainly for the BBC. This is Sarah's first theatre production.

Philip Ralph Writer

Philip wrote and developed *Mr Nobody* as part of Soho Theatre's Writer's Attachment Programme 2002. His previous plays (currently unproduced) are *Spilt Milk* and *The Running Man*. He is currently working on his next piece, provisionally entitled *Hitting Funny*. Philip trained in acting at the Royal Academy of Dramatic Art and his acting credits include seasons at Colchester, Scarborough and Stoke on Trent. He has played *Romeo, Lago* and *MacHeath* on tour nationally and third molly from the left in *Mother Clap's Molly House* (National Theatre and West End). On television he has played a wide variety of Yorkshire policemen.

Johanna Town Lighting Designer

Johanna Town has been Head of Lighting at the Royal Court Theatre since 1990, and has designed extensively for the company over that period, most recently *Under the Whaleback* and *Terrorism*. Johanna's lighting designs include over one hundred shows that have performed world-wide from London's West End to Australasier. Designs for 2003 include *She Stoops to Conquer* and *A Laughing Matter* (Out Of Joint, RNT) and *Brassed Off* (Liverpool Playhouse/Birmingham Rep). Johanna is very pleased to be back at Soho Theatre after designing *Modern Dance* (2002).

● soho
● theatre company

Soho is passionate in its commitment to new writing, producing a year-round programme of bold, original and accessible new plays – many of them from first-time playwrights.

'a foundry for new talent... one of the country's leading producer's of new writing' Evening Standard

Soho aims to be the first port of call for the emerging writer and is the only theatre to combine the process of production with the process of development. The unique Writers' Centre invites writers at any stage of their career to submit scripts and receives, reads and reports on over 2,000 per year. In addition to the national Verity Bargate Award – a competition aimed at new writers – it runs an extensive series of programmes from the innovative Under 11's Scheme, Young Writers Group (14-25s) and Westminster Prize (encouraging local writers) to a comprehensive Workshop Programme and Writers' Attachment Scheme working to develop writers not just in the theatre but also for radio, TV and film.

a creative hotbed... not only the making of theatre but the cradle for new screenplay and television scripts The Times

Contemporary, comfortable, air-conditioned and accessible, the Soho Theatre is busy from early morning to late at night. Alongside the production of new plays, it's also an intimate venue to see leading comedians from the UK and US in an eclectic programme mixing emerging new talent with established names. Soho Theatre is home to Café Lazeez, serving delicious Indian fusion dishes downstairs or, upstairs, a lively, late bar with a 1am licence.

'London's coolest theatre by a mile' Midweek

Soho Theatre Company is developing its work outside of the building, producing in Edinburgh and on tour in the UK whilst expanding the scope of its work with writers. It hosts the annual Soho Writers' Festival – now in its third year which brings together innovative practitioners from the creative industries with writers working in theatre, film, TV, radio, literature and poetry. Our programme aims to challenge, entertain and inspire writers and audiences from all backgrounds.

● soho
● theatre company

Soho Theatre and Writers' Centre

21 Dean Street, London W1D 3NE
Admin: 020 7287 5060 Fax: 020 7287 5061
Box Office: 020 7478 0100 Minicom: 020 7478 0136
www.sohotheatre.com   email: box@sohotheatre.com

Bars and Restaurant

Café Lazeez brasserie serves Indian-fusion dishes until 12pm. Late bar
open until 1am. The Terrace serves a range of soft and alcoholic drinks.

Email information list

For free regular programme updates and offers, join our free email
information list by emailing box@sohotheatre.com
If you would like to make any comments about any of the productions
seen at Soho Theatre, why not visit our chatroom at
www.sohotheatre.com?

Hiring the theatre

Soho Theatre has a range of rooms and spaces for hire. Please contact
the theatre managers on 020 7287 5060 or email hires@sohotheatre.com
for further details.

● soho
● theatre company

Artistic Director: Abigail Morris
Assistant to Artistic Director: Sarah Addison
Administrative Producer: Mark Godfrey
Assistant to Administrative Producer: Tim Whitehead
Acting Literary Manager: Jo Ingham
Associate Directors: Jonathan Lloyd, Tessa Walker
Casting Director: Ginny Schiller
Marketing and Development Director: Zoe Reed
Development Officer: Gayle Rogers
Marketing Director: Isabelle Sporidis
Marketing Officer: Ruth Waters
Marketing and Development Assistant: Kelly Duffy
Press Officer: Martin Shippen (020 7478 0142)
General Manager: Catherine Thornborrow
Acting General Manager: Jacqui Gellman
Front of House and Building Manager: Anne Mosley
Financial Controller: Kevin Dunn
Finance Officer: Hakim Oreagba
Box Office Manager: Kate Truefitt
Deputy Box Office Manager: Steve Lock
Box Office Assistants: Darren Batten, Wendy Buckland, Richard Gay,
Brett McCallum, Leah Read, William Sherriff Hammond, Natalie Worrall
and Miranda Yates
Duty Managers: Morag Brownlie, Mike Owen and Kate Ryan
Front of House Staff: Helene Le Bohec, Adam Buckles, Sharon Degen,
Meg Fisher, Claire Fowler, Sioban Hyams, Grethe Jensen, Sam Laydon,
Clair Randall, Katherine Smith, Rebecca Storey, Esme Sumsion, Luke
Tebbutt, Claire Townend, and Jamie Zubairi

THE SOHO THEATRE DEVELOPMENT CAMPAIGN

Soho Theatre Company receives core funding from Westminster City Council and London Arts. In order to provide as diverse a programme as possible and expand our audience development and outreach work, we rely upon additional support from trusts, foundations, individuals and corporates.

All our major sponsors share a common commitment to developing new areas of activity and encouraging creative partnerships between business and the arts.

If you would like to find out more about supporting Soho Theatre, please contact Gayle Rogers, Development Officer on 020 7478 0111 or email gayle@sohotheatre.com.

We are immensely grateful to all of our sponsors and donors for their support and commitment.

Sponsors: Bloomberg, Getty Images, TBWA\GGT

MR NOBODY

First published in 2003 by Oberon Books Ltd.
(incorporating Absolute Classics)
521 Caledonian Road, London N7 9RH
Tel: 020 7607 3637 / Fax: 020 7607 3629
e-mail: oberon.books@btinternet.com
www.oberonbooks.com

A catalogue record for this book is available from the British
Library.

ISBN: 1 84002 380 5

Cover photograph: Colin Hawkins / Getty Images

Printed in Great Britain by Antony Rowe Ltd, Chippenham.

for Fern

Acknowledgements

My thanks to: Jonathan, Abigail, Jo and everybody at Soho; Ruth Little; my fellow writers on attachment: Peggy, Mark, Neela and Antonia; the cast: Niall, Patricia and Maggie; Toby Whithouse; Karl Johnson; Sophie Stanton; Robin Soans; Hettie McDonald; and all my friends who have read my work over the last two years and given me their thoughts and encouragement.

The text is accurate to the first week of rehearsal.

Characters

JEAN
late 30s. A social worker

TOMMY
late 50s. A tramp

CLAIRE
late 50s. A housewife

Notes

The time is the present.
The setting is an attic storage room
in a church hall in a large city.
The play is one scene to be played in real time
with no interval.
An oblique / stroke in a speech serves as the cue
for the next speaker to overlap the first.

Darkness.

The muted sound of traffic and children playing.

After a few moments, a door opens stage left and light streams into the room, throwing the shadow of JEAN across the floor. She stands for a moment and tries the light switch. Nothing. She tries it again a few times. She curses under her breath.

She enters the room, puts her bag down on the floor in the beam of light and disappears into the darkness at the back of the room. We can hear her muttered exclamations as she blunders in the darkness, looking for something.

Presently a curtain stage right is thrown open and daylight spills into the room. It is an attic storage room in the eaves of a church hall. It was clearly once used a great deal – there are faded children's paintings on the walls, notices and posters – but it has not been in use for some time. There are piles of boxes stacked in corners, piles of chairs, folding tables. There are cobwebs here and there and dust in the air.

JEAN releases the blind covering the skylight upstage right and the room is now bathed in the light of a grey, overcast day. The street noise gets louder. She comes back to the centre of the room and looks around. A smile plays around her lips. She is a social worker. A striking woman in her late thirties. Shoulder length hair, smart trouser suit, her bag is full of files, and she carries a handbag and a take away coffee. She looks more closely at some of the children's pictures, tears a couple off the wall to reveal some painted over graffiti which has been etched into the wall. She smiles.

She takes a chair from one of the piles and places it facing the open door. She takes a second and places it facing the first with its back to the door. Pause. She takes a third and places it between the other two facing downstage. She thinks for a moment and replaces the third chair on the pile.

17

As she does so TOMMY enters behind her and stands in the doorway. He is a tramp in his late fifties, very scruffy and dirty, unkempt hair, beard, black hands and fingernails, old, dirty and torn clothes. He is carrying a bag of Big Issues.

JEAN finishes replacing the chair and turns back into the room, seeing TOMMY.

Pause.

JEAN smiles in welcome. He just looks at her blankly. It is clearly an uncomfortable moment.

JEAN: You look well.

> *Pause.*

> Well, you look better than the last time I saw you.

TOMMY: That wouldn't be difficult.

JEAN: No.

TOMMY: I've got some amazing scars.

JEAN: I'm sure.

TOMMY: It can no longer be said that I have no distinguishing marks.

> *Pause.*

> Did they ever catch them?

JEAN: Who?

TOMMY: The ones who attacked me.

JEAN: Oh. I don't believe so.

TOMMY: No.

> *Beat.*

> You look different.

JEAN: Do I?

TOMMY: Yes, your hair's longer.

JEAN: Well, it has been a year.

TOMMY: Suits you.

JEAN: Thank you.

TOMMY: Has it really been a year?

JEAN: Just over.

TOMMY: Feels longer.

JEAN: Does it?

> *Pause.*

Have you remembered anything?

TOMMY: No.

JEAN: Nothing?

TOMMY: Not the proverbial dickie bird.

> *Beat.*

The only thing I remember before that night is Pinball Wizard.

> *Beat.*

JEAN: So, nothing's come back?

TOMMY: Nothing.

> *Beat.*

JEAN: Still, I suppose if Pinball Wizard is in there, there must be other memories too. Somewhere.

TOMMY: I suppose so.

> *Beat.*

Hardly the most useful thing I could have remembered though.

JEAN: No.

Pause.

TOMMY: So, you wanted to see me.

JEAN: Yes. Thanks for coming.

TOMMY: My pleasure.

JEAN: It's nice to see you again.

JEAN extends her hand to TOMMY. He hesitates for a moment before taking her hand and shaking.

TOMMY: And you.

JEAN: Would you like to sit down?

TOMMY: Thank you.

They sit.

JEAN: I just wanted to catch up with you and see how you were getting on.

TOMMY: I'm doing fine.

JEAN: You're surviving.

TOMMY: As well as anyone, yeah.

JEAN: But anyone doesn't have your particular problem, do they?

TOMMY: No, but…I've been like this as long as I can remember.

Pause.

JEAN: Are you still happy at the hostel?

TOMMY: Yes, it's fine.

JEAN: Are you sure?

TOMMY: It's a nice place to stay and the people are friendly.

JEAN: Tommy, it's a horrible place to stay and the people are violent and aggressive.

TOMMY: Well, you can't have everything.

Beat.

JEAN: I know you haven't been there in months.

Pause.

Why didn't you come to me?

TOMMY: I didn't want to bother you.

JEAN: You wouldn't have been…

TOMMY: I just wanted some peace and quiet. I couldn't hear myself think in there. There's always noise and screaming and I just wanted quiet.

JEAN: I could have found you somewhere quiet.

TOMMY: No, you couldn't.

JEAN: Well, quieter.

TOMMY: Why should I be your responsibility? I'm a grown man.

JEAN: A grown man with no idea who he is.

TOMMY: I'm not your problem.

JEAN: You're not a problem.

Beat.

Where have you been sleeping?

TOMMY: Around.

Beat.

Parks mostly. They're usually the quietest places. I can think there.

JEAN: Will you let me help you find somewhere else to live?

TOMMY: No.

JEAN: Why not?

TOMMY: Because it's not your job.

JEAN: It is my job.

Beat.

TOMMY: You know, one of the most extraordinary things about amnesia isn't the things you can't remember. It's the things you can't forget.

Beat.

I remember everything about the last year down to the tiniest detail. I remember waking up in the hospital. I remember meeting you...and I remember you telling me that your specific job was to help people find a place to stay when they've been discharged from hospital.

Beat.

And nothing else.

Pause.

I was discharged twelve months ago.

JEAN: This is just a follow up interview.

TOMMY: I don't believe you.

Beat.

Why did you come looking for me, Jean?

Pause. TOMMY takes a piece of food from his pocket. It is wrapped in paper and he unwraps it. It is clearly repulsive.

JEAN: Tommy, you can't eat that.

He looks at JEAN and takes a big bite. He takes his time to chew and swallow.

TOMMY: What's this all about?

JEAN: I'd hoped that we could have a chat, just to catch up on how you've been getting on and to see if there's anything I can do to help you.

TOMMY: Why?

JEAN: Why what?

TOMMY: Why do you want to help me?

JEAN: I can offer you support, someone to talk to…

TOMMY: I'm doing fine.

JEAN: Not from where I'm sitting.

TOMMY: Then sit somewhere else.

Silence.

Anyway, you can't help me…even if you want to. You're a social worker. Not a neurologist.

Pause.

Look, I'm…not used to people…people don't usually go out of their way to help me…so I can get a bit defensive sometimes.

JEAN: And paranoid?

TOMMY: Who says that about me?

Beat.

Okay, yeah, I can get a bit paranoid. But wouldn't you, in my position?

JEAN: I'm sure I would, yes.

Pause.

You didn't go to see the psychologist.

TOMMY: No.

JEAN: Why not?

TOMMY: I don't believe in all that bollocks.

JEAN: I see.

Pause.

TOMMY: Look, Jean, I appreciate you'd like to help me but…it's been over a year. Nothing's come back to me. I don't know who I am. I'm nobody. I'm a nobody called Tommy. And that's that.

JEAN: And that's enough for you?

TOMMY: Of course not. But it's all I've got.

JEAN: Surely you'd still like to know who you are?

TOMMY: Maybe I would. But you aren't my fairy godmother and I can't see your wand anywhere so it looks like it isn't my lucky day, doesn't it?

Pause.

JEAN: In the hospital, when I asked you if you'd like me to register you as missing, you said no.

Beat.

You said nobody would miss you.

Beat.

Do you remember that?

TOMMY: Course I do.

Beat.

Nobody has missed me. I think I would have spotted a national campaign to find me. So… I mustn't be worth looking for.

JEAN: Is that what you really think?

TOMMY: Yeah.

Beat.

Maybe. I don't know.

JEAN: So, how would you feel if somebody did come looking for you?

Beat.

TOMMY: Depends who.

JEAN: Your wife. For example.

Beat.

TOMMY: I'd be pleased, naturally.

JEAN: Would you?

TOMMY: Of course. She could tell me who I am.

JEAN: And she would have missed you. And that would mean you were worth missing, wouldn't it?

Pause.

TOMMY: What are you getting at?

JEAN: I'm simply trying to establish how you would feel if someone came looking for you.

TOMMY: Why?

JEAN: Because someone's come looking for you.

Beat.

TOMMY: Who?

JEAN: Your wife.

Pause.

TOMMY: I don't understand.

JEAN: Your wife has come looking for you.

TOMMY: No, I…I understand that bit. What I don't understand is how…how did she find me?

JEAN: Through the National Missing Persons helpline.

TOMMY: But I wasn't registered as a Missing Person.

JEAN: Yes, you were.

TOMMY: How?

JEAN: I registered you.

Beat.

It was my professional judgement that at the time you were in no fit state to make rational decisions and that it would be wholly appropriate for you to be registered.

TOMMY: But I asked you not to.

JEAN: I'm aware of that. But under / the circumstances

TOMMY: You had no right to do that! I don't care about your professional judgement! I didn't want…you should have respected my decision.

JEAN: I did.

TOMMY: You've a funny way of showing it!

JEAN: I respected your decision. But I also recognised that it would be in your best interests to ignore your decision.

TOMMY: I'm not a child, y'know.

JEAN: I thought you wanted to find out who you are.

TOMMY: I do!

JEAN: Then what's the problem?

TOMMY: It's not against the law to go missing!

Pause.

JEAN: I'm aware of that. In fact, if you remember, and I'm
sure you do, I informed you of that when we met.

Beat.

I'm not accusing you of having committed a crime.

TOMMY: Then what are you accusing me of?

JEAN: I'm not accusing you of anything.

TOMMY: Well, it sounds like you are!

JEAN: Okay, listen, let's just…let's be absolutely clear
about this so there are no grounds for confusion. At the
time you were admitted to hospital you were in a highly
delicate state. You'd been attacked. You had severe stab
wounds to your chest and trauma to your head. You
claimed to have no memory / before that evening.

TOMMY: Claimed!?

JEAN: Just let me finish! You claimed to have no memory
before that evening and after extensive tests they found
no evidence of injury to your brain. Consequently there
is no medical way of proving that you do indeed have
amnesia.

TOMMY: Are you saying I'm lying?

JEAN: No.

TOMMY: Why would I lie?

JEAN: I don't know and I'm not saying you are! I'm simply saying that if you are lying then it's your business and it's certainly not a crime.

Beat.

I took the decision to register you against your wishes. I apologise for that. But I certainly don't apologise for the fact that, because I took that decision, you are now in a position to know who you are. And return to your life.

Beat.

If you want to.

Silence.

TOMMY: I wake up every morning and it takes me an hour to remember that I don't know who I am. I try to cling onto my dreams in case they might tell me something but they're gone before I open my eyes. It's taken me a year to discover even a fraction of the things that you take for granted. What I like and don't like, what I eat, what I'm allergic to. A thousand little decisions every day completely stump me…because I don't know what I would do.

Beat.

And you sit there and tell me that you don't believe me.

JEAN: Whether I believe you or not isn't important. What / matters –

TOMMY: It's important to me.

JEAN: What matters is that your wife has come forward and you have the chance to return to your life.

TOMMY: If I want to.

JEAN: If you want to.

Beat.

TOMMY: So, this is the real reason I'm here?

JEAN: Of course.

Beat.

I felt that a face-to-face discussion would be the best way to explain it to you and…well, I wasn't sure that you would come if you knew the truth.

Beat.

I apologise if I misled you.

TOMMY: Better late than never.

Pause.

JEAN: Since I was the person who registered you and the last person to have contact with you, I was the first port of call when your wife came forward. I agreed to arrange this meeting.

TOMMY: But it isn't your job, is it?

JEAN: That's correct. In fact, there is no statutory provision for this kind of situation which is…rare, to say the least.

Beat.

TOMMY: So, if it isn't your job and you don't have to be doing it…

JEAN: If I don't, nobody will.

Beat.

It's that simple.

Beat.

TOMMY: I'm not lying.

Beat.

It's important to me that you know that because it's the only truth I've got.

JEAN: I understand.

TOMMY: So, you've met her? My...my wife.

JEAN: I have, yes. On two occasions.

TOMMY: And she knows who I am.

JEAN: She does.

TOMMY: So, you know who I am.

JEAN: I do.

Beat.

Your name is Graham. Graham Wilson. Your wife's name is Claire.

Silence.

TOMMY: Bloody hell.

JEAN: Does it mean anything to you? Does anything...does it help you to remember?

Pause.

TOMMY: No.

Beat.

So...what's the next step? What happens now?

JEAN: That's entirely up to you. You don't have to see her if you don't want to. If that's what you want then, of course, you're free to go and I'll pass on your wishes to Claire.

Beat.

However if you do want to see her then you have two options. You can arrange through me a mutually convenient time for the two of you to meet in the future…

TOMMY: Or?

JEAN: Or you can see her now.

Beat.

TOMMY: She's here?

JEAN: Downstairs.

Beat.

It's quite a journey for her to get here and I couldn't rely on being able to find you twice so…I asked her to come. But, let me reiterate that you are under absolutely no obligation to see her and should you wish me to…are you alright?

TOMMY: I can't breathe.

He is struggling for breath.

JEAN: What's wrong?

TOMMY: I don't know…I…just…can't breathe.

JEAN: Okay, it's okay. Just try to relax.

TOMMY: I think…I need…to lie down.

JEAN: Okay, here we go.

She helps him to the floor.

Just try and keep your breathing slow and steady. Are you asthmatic?

TOMMY: How…should…I…know?

JEAN: Okay, try to relax, Tommy, keep breathing, slow and steady, slow and steady.

She retrieves the paper bag her coffee came in.

Just breathe into this bag for me. That's it. Over the nose as well. That's good. Long, slow, steady breaths.

He calms.

That's it. That's good. It's okay, you're okay.

His breathing gradually returns to normal.

TOMMY: Sorry.

JEAN: It's fine. What happened?

TOMMY: I don't know. I just couldn't breathe.

JEAN: Don't try and get up, just stay there a minute.

Pause.

TOMMY: I can't see her now.

JEAN: Why not?

TOMMY: Look at me! Just look at me! I can't! What will she think? I'm filthy, I smell awful, I'm hardly a prize catch, am I? I…

JEAN: No, but…okay, just breathe into the bag. That's good.

Beat.

Really Tommy, she won't care how you look or how you smell. You're her husband.

Pause.

It's your decision. I'm not going to force you to see her and I've made it clear to her that she can't force you either. It's entirely up to you.

Pause.

What do you think?

TOMMY: Doesn't seem like I have much of a choice, does it?

JEAN: Of course, you've got a choice.

TOMMY: Really? So I can just walk out of here, can I?

JEAN: If that's what you want.

Pause.

TOMMY: So, she's downstairs, is she?

JEAN: Yes.

Beat.

TOMMY: I suppose I'd better see her then. Since she's come all this way.

JEAN: Great. That's great.

Beat.

Thank you.

Pause.

TOMMY: And we'll meet here, will we? In this room?

JEAN: If that's okay with you.

Beat.

TOMMY: It's fine.

JEAN: I felt it was important that it was a neutral space, y'know, somewhere that held no history for either of you but that wasn't official or soulless.

TOMMY: Yes, I see.

Beat.

Do you use this place a lot for...this kind of thing?

JEAN: No. Never. I...well...I used to come to youth club here when I was young.

TOMMY: I see.

JEAN: I went to the school across the road. My mum lives near here. I'm...staying with her at the moment

TOMMY: So, it's a trip down memory lane.

Beat. She goes to the graffiti.

JEAN: I did that when I was twelve.

TOMMY: What does it say? I can't...

JEAN: It says 'Jean 4 David 4 Ever'.

TOMMY: David?

JEAN: David Cassidy.

Beat.

TOMMY: It didn't work out between you, then?

Pause.

JEAN: Are you feeling better now?

TOMMY: I think so.

JEAN: Can you get up?

TOMMY: Yes.

She helps him to the chair.

Sorry about that. I don't know what happened there.

JEAN: It's fine. You don't have to do anything you don't want to.

TOMMY: Yes, I see that.

JEAN: And I'm sorry for all the subterfuge.

TOMMY: I understand.

Beat.

Difficult situation for you.

JEAN: Not nearly as difficult as it is for you.

Pause.

How do you feel?

TOMMY: Scared.

JEAN: Of course.

Beat.

It's very important that you understand that you don't have to make any decisions today. And don't worry if there's no instant recovery of your memory. It's absolutely fine if this is the first of many meetings.

TOMMY: Or the only one?

Beat.

JEAN: Yes, that's fine, too.

Pause.

There is one other thing I should tell you before I bring Claire in.

TOMMY: Yes?

Pause.

Is it that bad?

JEAN: No, it's not bad as such, it just may come as a bit of a shock.

TOMMY: Oh, God, any more shocks and I'll never recover my memory.

JEAN: This is the last one, I promise.

TOMMY: Don't make promises you can't keep.

Beat.

JEAN: The thing is…Claire…your wife tells me that you've actually been missing for a bit longer than a year.

TOMMY: How much longer?

Beat.

JEAN: Four years longer.

Pause.

TOMMY: I've been missing for five years?

JEAN: That's what she says.

TOMMY: You said a bit longer.

JEAN: Yes, well…

TOMMY: Five years?

JEAN: Yes.

Pause.

TOMMY: What have I been doing all that time?

JEAN: I'm sure we'd all like to know the answer to that question.

TOMMY: Nobody more than me.

Beat.

Five years.

JEAN: I'm sorry, Graham.

TOMMY: Please…don't call me that.

JEAN: It's your name.

TOMMY: I know, but…it's…it just feels strange…wrong, somehow.

JEAN: I'm sure it will for a while.

Pause.

Are you ready to meet her now?

TOMMY: I suppose so.

JEAN: I'll go and get her.

TOMMY: Thank you.

JEAN gets up to go.

Jean?

JEAN: Yes?

TOMMY: I'd like to see her alone.

Beat.

JEAN: Of course.

JEAN picks up her bag.

I'll be outside if you need me.

TOMMY: Thank you.

She takes his hand for a moment.

JEAN: Don't worry. I'm sure everything will be fine.

TOMMY: What have I told you about promises?

She smiles, releases his hand and goes.

TOMMY sits for a moment in the chair with his back to the door. Then he moves to the chair facing the door. He takes off his overcoat. He is wearing a very dirty Arsenal football shirt, which he takes off and puts into his bag. Underneath he is wearing a plain and relatively clean t-shirt. He puts his overcoat back on.

He sits. He stands. He sits again. He crosses his legs. He uncrosses them. Stands again. Sits again. Stands, walks away from the chairs to look out of the window. Faces the door, faces the window, faces the door, looks out of the window.

CLAIRE enters and stops in the doorway when she sees TOMMY. She is in her late fifties, very well kept, if plain. She waits. Eventually TOMMY turns. They look at each other. Long silence.

CLAIRE: Aren't you going to say hello then?

Beat.

TOMMY: Hello Claire.

CLAIRE: You remember me?

Pause. TOMMY shakes his head.

TOMMY: I'm sorry.

Beat.

CLAIRE: You look older.

TOMMY: Yes.

CLAIRE: Five years older.

TOMMY: So I hear.

Pause.

CLAIRE: You really don't remember me?

TOMMY: I'm sorry.

CLAIRE: Don't be sorry for that, Graham. Be sorry for leaving in the first place.

TOMMY: I'm sorry for that too.

CLAIRE: So you bloody should be.

Pause.

Well, come here then.

He goes to her. She looks intently at him. She puts her arms around him. She starts to cry but controls herself.

Where have you been all this time?

TOMMY: I don't know.

CLAIRE: I thought you were dead.

TOMMY: I'm sorry.

She pulls away a little and looks at him again. She kisses him. She stops.

CLAIRE: Aren't you going to kiss me back?

TOMMY: Sorry.

He kisses her.

CLAIRE: Oh, it is you. Thank God. I'd know that kiss anywhere.

TOMMY: You weren't sure before?

CLAIRE: Well, you looked a bit different in the photo and…

TOMMY: The photo?

CLAIRE: The one on the website.

TOMMY: Oh. I see.

Beat.

That's cause I'd been hurt.

CLAIRE: Yes, I know.

Pause.

Are you better now?

TOMMY: I think so. Apart from…y'know, my memory.

CLAIRE: Yes.

Beat.

What happened to you?

TOMMY: They think I was attacked.

CLAIRE: They think?

TOMMY: I don't remember.

Beat.

Anything.

Pause.

Is it me?

CLAIRE: It's you.

Beat.

My Graham.

TOMMY: Graham.

CLAIRE: They said you'd been calling yourself Tommy.

TOMMY: That's right.

CLAIRE: That's when I knew. Had to be you. You've always loved him.

Beat.

TOMMY: Pete Townshend?

CLAIRE: No, silly! Tommy Steele.

TOMMY: Tommy Steele?

CLAIRE: Yes. You've got all his records. We loved him in 'Singin' in the Rain'. Don't you remember?

Beat.

TOMMY: No.

CLAIRE: You took me for my birthday. It was wonderful.

TOMMY: That's nice.

CLAIRE: Yes. It was a lovely treat.

Beat.

You were always doing things like that. You used to say it was the easiest thing in the world to surprise me. And you loved to watch my face when I…when you…

She has started to cry.

TOMMY: Claire, I …

CLAIRE: I'm alright, I'll be alright.

She puts her arms around him and sobs. He holds her clumsily.

I've missed you…so much. It's been so long. I didn't know if I could take another day. The worry. The thought that you might be dead…or worse. They said…some of them said that you were but I never believed them, Gray, never! They said you'd left me for someone else but I knew that you'd rather die than do that to me. Oh, Gray.

She buries her head in his chest. Pause.

When was the last time you had a bath?

TOMMY: Quite a while.

CLAIRE: Smells like it. That's not like you.

TOMMY: Isn't it?

CLAIRE: No. Always clean you are. One of the first things I noticed about you.

TOMMY: I'm sorry.

CLAIRE: You need a good scrub.

TOMMY: Yes.

CLAIRE: You can have a nice long bath when I get you home.

Beat.

TOMMY: That'll be nice.

CLAIRE: Everything's just as you left it. I've kept the car running. Bob comes and takes me for a run most days. It's good for him to get out after…and I've kept all your clothes clean and ironed in your wardrobe, ready for you. You look like you've lost a bit of weight. They'll be hanging off you.

TOMMY: Claire.

CLAIRE: Bob's organising a welcome home do at the pub. Everyone'll be there. It's not just me that's missed you, y'see. They all have, the whole gang.

TOMMY: That's nice. Claire…

CLAIRE: I don't think we should tell people you've been selling that magazine, do you? I mean, I'm sure you've done what you had to but…people don't need to know, do they?

TOMMY: Claire!

Beat.

CLAIRE: What is it, Gray?

TOMMY: I don't remember you.

Beat.

CLAIRE: I know but…if you give it time…

TOMMY: No, I'm saying I don't remember you.

Pause.

CLAIRE: I don't…what do you mean? It's me, Gray, it's Claire. You must remember me.

TOMMY: I don't.

CLAIRE: But you must.

TOMMY: But I don't! I don't remember you at all. I don't remember ever seeing you before in my life. Do you understand?

CLAIRE: Don't you remember anything?

TOMMY: Of course I don't remember anything! I've got total amnesia! Is that so hard to comprehend, woman?

Pause.

I'm sorry.

CLAIRE: There's no need to shout at me, Graham.

TOMMY: I know, I'm sorry.

CLAIRE: It's very hard for me to understand, you know.

TOMMY: Yes. I'm sorry.

Pause.

CLAIRE: I thought you'd remember once you saw me.

TOMMY: Yes.

CLAIRE: Jean said that it's usually when someone sees their loved one for the first time that they snap out if it.

Beat.

I'm your loved one.

Pause.

TOMMY: I'm sorry.

Beat.

CLAIRE: I don't like her.

TOMMY: Who? Jean?

CLAIRE: Yes.

TOMMY: Neither did I when I first met her.

CLAIRE: There's something not right about her. All that fake sympathy and concern when you know she's only doing her job.

TOMMY: She isn't doing her job.

CLAIRE: Yes, she is, she…

TOMMY: This has nothing to do with her job. She's doing this…out of the kindness of her heart.

CLAIRE: Oh, I don't believe that for a second.

Beat.

There's something not right about her.

Pause.

TOMMY: I just don't remember you, Claire. I'm sorry.

CLAIRE: Oh, stop saying you're sorry, for God's sake. You're getting on my nerves.

Beat.

If you were that bloody sorry, you'd remember me.

TOMMY: I don't think that exactly follows.

CLAIRE: Well, just stop saying it.

Silence.

So…what do we do now?

TOMMY: I don't know.

Pause.

CLAIRE: What are you thinking?

Beat.

TOMMY: Nothing.

CLAIRE: No, come on, tell me.

TOMMY: No, it's…it's nothing.

CLAIRE: Graham, I have spent the last five years of my life waiting and praying that you would come back to me. The least you can do after all this time is tell me what you're thinking!

Beat.

TOMMY: I'm thinking that I'm sorry.

Pause.

CLAIRE: Would it help if I told you a bit about yourself?

TOMMY: What like?

CLAIRE: Things you like, things you don't like, who your friends are, that kind of thing.

Beat.

Do you think that would work?

TOMMY: It's got to be worth a try.

Pause.

CLAIRE: Where shall I start?

TOMMY: At the beginning.

Beat.

CLAIRE: We met at Bob and Alice's wedding.

TOMMY: Bob and Alice?

CLAIRE: You were best man, I was maid of honour.

TOMMY: How did I know Bob?

CLAIRE: From work. You started the business together. You'd been friends since school, you…

TOMMY: What kind of work do I do?

CLAIRE: You don't remember any of this?

Pause.

You were a plumber.

TOMMY: Were?

CLAIRE: You'd retired.

TOMMY: I'd retired?

CLAIRE: Yes, well the firm was doing well and after your heart scare we decided that you should take it early. So you could spend more time with me, you said. Didn't work out that way though.

Beat.

TOMMY: When was this?

CLAIRE: About six years ago.

TOMMY: No, I mean when we met.

CLAIRE: The wedding? Well, Alice and Bob had their Silver Wedding eighteen months ago, just before she…so I suppose it's getting on for…

TOMMY: Twenty-seven years.

CLAIRE: Must be.

Beat.

That's if you count the last five, of course.

Pause.

TOMMY: Long time.

CLAIRE: Yes.

Pause.

TOMMY: What about my family?

CLAIRE: Your family?

TOMMY: Yes, are my parents still around or any brothers or sisters?

CLAIRE: Gray…you don't have a family.

TOMMY: I don't have a family.

CLAIRE: No.

TOMMY: Just like that? I don't have one.

CLAIRE: Well, your dad died when you were little, in the war, and your mum had you adopted.

TOMMY: Then what about…

CLAIRE: You ran away from there when you were fifteen and you haven't been back since.

Beat.

TOMMY: So, no family then?

CLAIRE: No.

Beat.

Just me.

Pause. It starts to rain outside. Drops fall on the skylight.

TOMMY: Do we have any children?

CLAIRE: No.

TOMMY: Oh. Right.

Beat.

Why not?

CLAIRE: Because we can't have them.

TOMMY: Right. Sorry.

Pause.

What do I like?

CLAIRE: Me.

TOMMY: Apart from you.

CLAIRE: Lots of things. Cars, football, you like a drink.

TOMMY: Do I drink a lot?

CLAIRE: No more than anyone else.

TOMMY: How much is that?

CLAIRE: Well, a few pints a night and a bit more at the weekends. And you like a whisky to help you sleep. Normal, really.

TOMMY: Favourite food?

CLAIRE: Meat. Any kind. You like a good steak, and roast anything…pork, chicken, lamb…I can never get you to eat fish, apart from tuna. I'd always send you off with tuna sandwiches for your lunch. You couldn't get enough of them.

Beat.

I've got loads of chops in the freezer special for when you get home.

TOMMY: Thank you.

Beat.

What am I passionate about?

CLAIRE: Me.

TOMMY: No, I mean…other than you…hobbies, that kind of thing.

CLAIRE: The Gunners. You love the Arsenal. You used to joke that you loved them more than me. You used to be a season ticket holder but I had to let it go, Gray. It was so expensive.

TOMMY: Anything else?

CLAIRE: Soaps. You can't get enough of them. I have to tiptoe round when they're on.

Pause.

TOMMY: Am I a good man?

CLAIRE: Course you are, love.

TOMMY: No, I mean, am I good to you? Am I kind to you?

CLAIRE: We have our ups and downs but I can't complain. You have your moods but you wouldn't be human otherwise, would you?

TOMMY: Have I ever hit you?

CLAIRE: Never.

TOMMY: Really?

CLAIRE: Only when I deserve it. I can be a right clumsy cow sometimes.

Pause.

TOMMY: Do I love you?

CLAIRE: Your angel, that's what you call me.

TOMMY: Have I always been faithful to you?

CLAIRE: Of course you have.

Beat.

TOMMY: I haven't, have I?

CLAIRE: There was the one but…

TOMMY: Just the one?

CLAIRE: Yes! And you stopped it when I found out so it's all forgotten now.

TOMMY: I'm sorry.

Pause.

CLAIRE: You're a good man, Gray. You're my good man. We have a good life together. Honestly. I've waited for you. I've never wanted anyone else. I've had offers, don't think I haven't, but it's always been you for me and me for you and that's how we like it.

Pause.

Come home, love.

TOMMY: I still don't remember you, Claire.

CLAIRE: I don't care. You're my Graham. I want you to come home with me.

Pause.

TOMMY: I can't.

CLAIRE: Why not, Gray?

TOMMY: Because I don't know who you are.

CLAIRE: Oh, Gray…

TOMMY: My name is Tommy. That's the name I've given myself. I don't know who Graham is.

CLAIRE: But I do!

TOMMY: And am I supposed to just take your word for it? Because you say that's who I am, should I just believe you and come home with you?

CLAIRE: Yes!

TOMMY: Well, I can't.

Beat.

I'm sorry, Claire, I am. But how can I be someone I don't remember? And how can I live with someone I don't remember? I'm sorry for the last five years of your life. It must have been a very difficult time / for you but –

CLAIRE: Difficult? You don't know the first thing about difficult! It's easy for you. You just walked away and washed your hands of me!

TOMMY: I don't think / that's –

CLAIRE: I've held our life together without you for five years! I've kept our home together, without your pension, without anybody's help. If it weren't for Bob I wouldn't have been able to manage. The doctor's had me on pills to help me sleep. Some nights I've thought about ending it all! How can you sit there now and say you don't know me? How can you do it to me?

TOMMY: I'm sorry.

Beat.

I don't know what else to say except I'm sorry.

Pause.

Why wouldn't they give you my pension?

CLAIRE: What?

TOMMY: You said you've kept your home together without your husband's pension.

CLAIRE: Yes. That's…that's right.

TOMMY: Surely they should have just signed it over to you after he'd been gone for a year or so?

CLAIRE: No…there were…complications.

TOMMY: What kind of complications?

Beat.

CLAIRE: I don't know. I can barely understand half the stuff they tell me but…there were problems and so they couldn't give it to me.

TOMMY: But Bob's been helping you manage?

CLAIRE: Yes, we've…Alice got cancer and…so we've kept each other company. I don't know what I'd have done without him.

Pause.

TOMMY: I hate tuna, Claire.

CLAIRE: Do you?

TOMMY: I can't stand it. Every time I've been given a tuna sandwich I've almost been sick. I absolutely hate it.

CLAIRE: Well, my Graham loved it.

TOMMY: Did he?

CLAIRE: Yes, he…you did.

Silence. TOMMY goes to the door.

Gray?

TOMMY: Jean? Could you come in, please?

CLAIRE: What are you doing?

JEAN enters.

JEAN: How's it going?

Beat.

Graham?

TOMMY: My name isn't Graham.

CLAIRE: What d'you mean, Gray?

TOMMY: This woman is lying.

JEAN: What?

CLAIRE: Gray, how can you…

TOMMY: She isn't my wife.

CLAIRE: I am! It's true, Gray, you know it is. You are my…

TOMMY: No, I'm not and you know I'm not!

JEAN: Claire, Grah…Tommy, can we just calm down and talk this through.

TOMMY: No, I don't think we can.

TOMMY picks up his bag.

I hope you're better at your real job than you are at your hobby, Jean. You drag me here to meet some woman who claims to be my wife / when she clearly –

CLAIRE: I am!

TOMMY: – isn't. She says I love tuna and I hate tuna; she says that she can't get hold of her husband's pension when everybody knows that it would automatically go to her once he'd been declared dead. She's just some sad, old bag who's come out of the woodwork cos she doesn't want to be alone anymore!

JEAN: But have you actually remembered anything?

TOMMY: I don't need to know who I am to know I'm being lied to.

He starts to leave.

JEAN: Graham, where are you…

TOMMY: Back to my day job. Nice to meet you, Claire. Better luck next time.

TOMMY exits. JEAN runs after him.

JEAN: Graham! Tommy, please, wait, let's…at least let's try and talk it through! Tommy!

We hear JEAN following TOMMY down the stairs and out of earshot. Silence. CLAIRE sits quietly, shocked. She starts to cry. After a few moments, JEAN returns.

Claire, what…what happened? What did you say to him?

Pause.

Claire?

CLAIRE: I thought he might have changed. I thought after all this time things might have been different but they're just the same. Same as he always was.

JEAN: But he says that he…

CLAIRE: I don't care what he says! That's my Graham! This is just like him. There's always got to be games. Games and mess and fuss. I feel such a fool.

JEAN: Claire, you mustn't…it's not your fault. He…

CLAIRE: He loved tuna! He loved it. Couldn't get enough, never wanted any other kind of sandwich. Just tuna.

JEAN: Claire, I...I said that you had to prepare yourself for him not wanting to come back.

CLAIRE: And I did, but...I at least expected him to remember me!

JEAN: I know.

CLAIRE: Twenty-two years we were together.

JEAN: Yes.

CLAIRE: Twenty-two years.

Pause.

JEAN: I'm sorry.

Beat.

CLAIRE: It isn't your fault. You're only doing your job.

JEAN: Well, I...yes.

Pause. CLAIRE wipes her eyes.

CLAIRE: Can't we get him back? I'm sure if we talked about it, he...

JEAN: He's gone, Claire. I...he's very angry. Not with you, with me. He thinks he's been lied to. That I lied to him. We can't keep him here against his will. I'm sorry.

CLAIRE: Oh, God.

CLAIRE starts to cry again.

JEAN: Claire, it's...it's okay, it'll be okay.

CLAIRE: No, it won't, you can't just say that, it won't!

JEAN: Well, it...I...

Pause. JEAN searches in her bag for a tissue and hands it to CLAIRE. CLAIRE wipes her eyes again.

CLAIRE: Thank you.

Beat.

JEAN: What happened while I was out of the room? What did you talk about?

CLAIRE: We... Oh, I don't know, everything. We talked about...he said that he didn't remember me, and I offered to tell him about himself and he said that might help.

JEAN: And did you tell him about the pension?

CLAIRE: I suppose I must have mentioned it.

JEAN: You never mentioned it to me.

CLAIRE: Well, it didn't seem important.

JEAN: It is.

Beat.

Why can't you access his pension, Claire?

CLAIRE: I don't know. There were complications.

JEAN: What kind of complications?

CLAIRE: Oh, I don't understand them. They said...they said that there were complications and they couldn't let me have the money, that's all.

JEAN: That's all they said?

CLAIRE: Well, it was all legal mumbo-jumbo...

JEAN: Do you have the letters?

CLAIRE: Letters?

JEAN: From the solicitor. I could have a look at them and maybe...

CLAIRE: No, I…I didn't keep them.

JEAN: I see.

Pause.

The trouble with that is, Claire…well, let's say that we can persuade him to meet with you again, I mean, we might not even be able to find him now…then we're going to need to be able to prove to him that he is who you say he is. And those letters would have been very important.

CLAIRE: Well, I didn't keep them.

JEAN: Fine.

Beat.

What about the things you do have? Papers, photographs, your marriage certificate…

CLAIRE: No.

JEAN: No? What d'you…surely you've kept something?

CLAIRE: No.

JEAN: Did you…what did you…you didn't throw it all away?

CLAIRE: No.

JEAN: So, what…

CLAIRE: There never were any.

Beat.

JEAN: But surely you must have…

CLAIRE: We were never married.

Pause.

We never got married so there never was a marriage certificate.

Beat.

There's nothing.

Pause.

JEAN: You told me he was your husband.

CLAIRE: He is.

JEAN: But you were never married!

CLAIRE: I spent twenty-two years of my life with him. That's what matters. Not a piece of paper.

JEAN: Is that why you can't access his pension? I mean, after twenty-two years...doesn't that make you...

CLAIRE: His common law wife, yes.

JEAN: So, surely...

CLAIRE: Some legal loophole, I told you, I don't understand it.

Pause.

JEAN: Claire, you're wearing a ring on your wedding finger.

CLAIRE: I know.

JEAN: It's why I never thought...I never questioned...

CLAIRE: I bought it myself.

Beat.

On the second anniversary of him...disappearing. It's costume jewellery. All I could afford.

Pause.

JEAN: It's nice.

CLAIRE: Thank you.

Pause.

Every Valentine's day I'd ask him and every year his answer would be the same, 'Maybe next year.' But he never changed his mind. 'What do we need to get married for? We're happy enough, aren't we? We love each other, don't we? What difference would a ring on your finger make? It would only mess up my tax.'

Pause.

JEAN: Why didn't you tell me this when you came forward?

CLAIRE: I thought you wouldn't believe me.

Beat.

JEAN: I do.

CLAIRE: Thank you.

Pause.

JEAN: Well, what about a photo?

CLAIRE shakes her head.

No?

CLAIRE: I haven't got any.

JEAN: Come on, Claire, you must have! Everybody takes photos. You can't tell me you haven't got one picture of him!

CLAIRE: Oh, yes, we had a few. Not good ones mind, he always hated having his picture taken. He'd always scowl or blink at the wrong time or turn away. But there were a few.

JEAN: So what happened to them?

Pause.

CLAIRE: He tore himself out of them all. The day he left. All of them. Every picture I had of him was gone. Even the one of us taken the day we met at Alice and Bob's wedding. In the frame over the fireplace. Gone.

Beat.

He'd even been into my purse and taken the one of him I had in there.

Pause.

JEAN: Your friends? Surely they…

CLAIRE: They had a few. But he was always hiding his face. Or offering to take the picture. Or moving at the last second. You wouldn't know it was him in any of them.

CLAIRE reaches into her bag and takes out an old, battered photograph. She looks at it for a moment before handing it to JEAN.

That's the only one. Bob found it in a drawer.

JEAN: I…which one… I can't see…

CLAIRE: Third from the left, back row.

Beat.

It's him and Bob when they were at school.

JEAN: This must be…how old is this?

CLAIRE: Forty years. Give or take.

Pause.

JEAN: Oh, Claire.

CLAIRE: I don't want your pity, Jean.

Silence. JEAN hands the photo back to CLAIRE.

JEAN: This makes things much more complicated.

CLAIRE: Not for me.

Silence. JEAN stands and goes to the window. CLAIRE takes her compact out of her bag and redoes her makeup.

JEAN: When we spoke…when we met and we talked about…well, talked about your marriage…was there anything else you didn't tell me?

CLAIRE: Like what?

JEAN: Well, you tell me.

Beat.

CLAIRE: No, I don't think so.

Pause.

JEAN: It's just…you said…you told me that you had a very happy…that you and Graham were very happy together.

CLAIRE: That's right.

Beat.

JEAN: Yes, well…if you'll forgive me for saying so…some of the things you've just told me have made me think that might not be the whole story.

CLAIRE: What things?

JEAN: Well, the…the fact that Graham didn't want to marry you and…

CLAIRE: I never said that.

JEAN: You…yes, you did…you…

CLAIRE: I said that I always asked him on Valentine's Day. And he always said no. But he did want to marry me. We were always just putting it off.

JEAN: He asked you to marry him?

CLAIRE: Often.

JEAN: But you just said…you had to buy your own ring…so…

CLAIRE: My husband disappeared.

JEAN: Yes, but…

CLAIRE: He loves me very much.

JEAN: Claire…

CLAIRE: He loves me very much.

Beat.

JEAN: Of course.

Pause.

Sorry to keep going on about this, Claire, but I'm just…

CLAIRE: Oh, it's fine. I'm sure you need to be thorough.

Beat.

JEAN: What I'm trying to get at here is…well, you said that you were very happy together and…I thought that you should have the chance to be that happy again…even if he's lost his memory he's still the same man and…maybe if you could go back…to the way things were before then…things would be alright again but…the way things were before wasn't very happy, was it, Claire?

Pause.

CLAIRE: That man is my Graham.

JEAN: I believe you, Claire, but…

CLAIRE: Who do you think you are? How dare you sit there and judge me…judge us? You don't know me and you don't know Gray. It's not up to you to sit there and tell me that we didn't love each other. That we don't love each other.

JEAN: Oh, I wasn't, I…I never said you didn't love each other.

CLAIRE: No, but that's what you were implying, wasn't it?

JEAN: I…

CLAIRE: I'm not stupid, Jean. I know I must seem to you like just another sad and lonely housewife, just another case file, but you don't know the first thing about me or my life. That man is my life, do you understand? He's my life. Are you married?

JEAN: Am I…?

CLAIRE: Yes, you. Are you married?

JEAN: Well, I…I'm separated, actually.

CLAIRE: Oh, I see. Recently?

Beat.

JEAN: Yes.

CLAIRE: What happened?

JEAN: Well, we aren't here to talk about me.

CLAIRE: No, but we are here to talk about me and I'm asking you what happened.

Beat.

JEAN: Well, we…he…it's complicated. I…

CLAIRE: In what way?

JEAN: Claire, I…

CLAIRE: No, I'd like an answer. In what way is it complicated?

Beat.

JEAN: There were some changes…well, I'd changed quite a lot and…

CLAIRE: And so he left you.

JEAN: I left him, as a matter of fact.

CLAIRE: He'd cheated on you.

JEAN: Of course not!

CLAIRE: So why did you leave him?

Pause.

JEAN: I don't know.

Beat.

Look, I'd really prefer it if we didn't talk about me, I…

CLAIRE: And I'd prefer it if we didn't talk about me but it seems that I have to. And now you know how it feels.

Beat.

I could say to you that you're in no position to judge me or my marriage if you can't even make your own work…but I won't do that, because I won't treat you the way you're treating me. No marriage is a bed of roses. But this is my marriage that we're talking about. My husband. If things were tough sometimes, that's our business. But I love him and he loves me. End of story.

Beat.

So, I would ask you, please, to treat me and my life with the same respect you would want for your own.

JEAN: Of course. Claire, I didn't mean...

CLAIRE: I'm sure you didn't.

Pause.

JEAN: I apologise.

CLAIRE: Thank you.

Silence.

CLAIRE: You're not the first, you know. Everyone has tried to persuade me to move on, put him behind me. Asking me if we were really that happy. But we were. We were.

JEAN: I know, Claire, I'm sure you were but...five years. How did you cope?

CLAIRE: Badly.

Pause.

I made a life with Graham. That's not an easy thing to throw away.

JEAN: But you've been living without that life for a long time.

CLAIRE: I wouldn't call it living.

Pause.

JEAN: Claire, even if we can persuade him he really is Graham...he still may not want to come back with you.

Beat.

You know that, don't you?

CLAIRE: He will.

JEAN: How can you be so sure?

CLAIRE: Look at his life.

Pause.

JEAN: Are you absolutely certain that he is Graham?

CLAIRE: How can you ask me that?

JEAN: Claire, I…

CLAIRE: That's like asking me how I know who I am. I know because I know. Because I feel like me. Because when I look in a mirror, I see me.

Beat.

When I walked into this room, I was looking at Graham. And I knew it was him because it felt like him and I could see him standing in front of me.

Pause.

There has to be a way to help him remember.

JEAN: If there is I'm afraid I don't know what it is.

CLAIRE: I've waited so long.

JEAN: I know.

CLAIRE: I've cleaned the house up special. I've got a lovely meal ready for him – all his favourites. I've made him a cake.

JEAN: That's nice.

CLAIRE: I've told everyone he knows. They're all waiting for him to come home. I can't…what will I say to them… I couldn't face them if…

She is crying again.

I can't go back there without him, Jean. I've…I've been so lonely. Nobody understands what I've been through.

JEAN: I know.

JEAN takes a tissue from her bag and hands it to CLAIRE.

CLAIRE: It's just…thank you…no word, nothing. He didn't even leave me a note. He was just gone. Like he'd never existed. Every day. Every day I expected him to walk back through the door. As if he'd never been away.

TOMMY enters, quietly, behind CLAIRE. JEAN sees him but makes no sign. CLAIRE continues, oblivious to his presence.

I at least thought he might phone. All this time, the last five years, thinking it was me…something I'd done…something I'd said…did I drive him away? Was it all my fault? I need him to come home, Jean. Do you understand? I need him to come home.

CLAIRE sees JEAN look over her shoulder. She turns to look at TOMMY. She gets up, goes to him and puts her arms around him. She cries into his chest. Pause.

You came back.

Pause. She looks at him.

You came back.

TOMMY: It's raining.

CLAIRE slaps TOMMY hard across the face and goes to the door.

JEAN: Claire…wait…please…

CLAIRE: I'm just going to…powder my…bathroom?

JEAN: Down the stairs. On the right. Third door.

CLAIRE: Thank you.

CLAIRE goes. TOMMY rubs his face, looks at JEAN.

TOMMY: Is she…

JEAN: What does it look like?

TOMMY: Well, don't blame me. It's not my fault.

JEAN: What isn't your fault?

Pause.

TOMMY: I don't remember her, Jean.

JEAN: Then why did you come back?

Pause.

TOMMY: Is she sure I'm him?

JEAN: Of course she is.

TOMMY: How can she be so sure?

JEAN: She spent twenty-two years with you.

TOMMY: With Graham.

JEAN: That's you.

TOMMY: And how can you be so sure?

JEAN: Because she is.

Beat.

Because I've just seen her trying not to let me see how heart broken she is, how much she needs you and misses you. How when you walked out of here, all her hopes went with you.

Pause.

TOMMY: I don't know what to do.

JEAN: I know.

TOMMY: I was standing out there, in the rain. Getting soaked. Thinking 'does it really matter if she's lying?' That can't be right can it? I mean, I've got to be able to

remember her, haven't I? I've got to be sure I'm
Graham, haven't I?

JEAN: Have you?

TOMMY: Of course I have. If I don't remember her and
still go with her…that's…what if I'm not him? What
then?

JEAN: What if you are?

Pause.

Tommy, look at yourself. Look at the way you've been
living. You sleep on the streets or in parks, you eat out of
bins, you survive by selling the…

TOMMY: There's nothing wrong with…

JEAN: I'm not saying there is but…given a choice. Are you
really telling me you'd prefer to stay as you are?

TOMMY: But if I don't remember her…

JEAN: Does it matter? She's a desperately lonely woman,
you're a desperately lonely man.

TOMMY: I'm not lonely!

JEAN: Yes, you are! And if you're trying to tell me that you
prefer it that way then I don't believe you.

Beat.

And if you're trying to tell me that you choose to be that
way then…I don't understand you.

Beat.

What harm could it do?

Pause.

TOMMY: I need some proof.

Beat.

JEAN: Fine. What kind of proof?

TOMMY: Oh, I don't know. Just proof, y'know.

Beat.

JEAN: Papers, documents…marriage certificate…?

TOMMY: That kind of thing.

Beat.

JEAN: I'm sure that wouldn't be a problem.

TOMMY: Good.

Pause.

JEAN: What about photographs?

Beat.

TOMMY: Of course. Photographs would be perfect.

JEAN: That's fine then.

Beat.

She's just been telling me about the albums she's got. In the wardrobe. Piles of them.

Pause.

TOMMY: That's okay then.

Pause.

JEAN: So…if she can prove it to you…even if you don't remember her…then would you be happy to go home with her?

TOMMY: Why is it so important to you?

JEAN: It isn't.

TOMMY: So, what's in it for you?

JEAN: Nothing's in it for me.

TOMMY: There must be something. You can't just be doing it for spiritual brownie points. So what is it?

JEAN: Look, I...Jesus! I'm just trying to help you. I thought you might want a chance to go back...to get your life back. It's not as if you've made a resounding success of it in the last five years, is it? I'm just trying to do a good turn! I'm beginning to wish I hadn't bothered!

TOMMY: Has it occurred to you that I might be happy?

Pause.

JEAN: No. That hadn't occurred to me.

Beat.

Do you want to know why that hadn't occurred to me?

TOMMY: Why?

JEAN: Because you aren't.

Silence. The rain stops.

Look, I...I wanted you to get back together.

Beat.

When I asked you here today. That's what I wanted.

Beat.

I left the social service. A couple of months ago. I resigned. So, I'm nobody official. And this really isn't my job.

Beat.

We all make mistakes.

Beat.

I've left my job. I've left my marriage. I've moved back in with my mum. I can't tell you what to do.

Beat.

We all deserve a second chance, Graham.

Pause.

TOMMY: Jean…what if…

JEAN: If ifs and ands were pots and pans…

Beat.

You won't know unless you try.

Pause.

And you wouldn't have come back if you didn't want to.

Beat.

Would you?

Pause. CLAIRE enters. Silence.

CLAIRE: I think it's stopped raining now. You can go.

Pause.

If that's all you came back in for then…

Silence.

Well, say something then, don't just stand there!

Pause.

I'm not going to let you do this to me, Gray. Not now. Not after five years.

Beat.

So…either you say something to me now…or I walk out of here…and I never come back.

Silence.

Do you hear me?

Silence. CLAIRE picks up her bag and turns to go.

Goodbye Jean.

CLAIRE is almost out of the door.

TOMMY: Claire.

Beat.

Please wait.

CLAIRE stops in the doorway and looks at TOMMY.

CLAIRE: Yes?

Pause.

TOMMY: Claire, I…I'm so very sorry.

Silence. CLAIRE walks to TOMMY and looks in his eyes.

I'm so very sorry, Claire.

CLAIRE: Oh, Gray…

They embrace. JEAN gets up quietly and exits. They hold each other for a long time. Both are emotional.

You remember me, then? You do, don't you?

Beat.

It's okay, we don't have to rush anything. It's okay.

TOMMY: It may take me a while, Claire, to…fully recover. I may not remember everything.

CLAIRE: I know, love. I don't mind. We'll get through it together.

TOMMY: You'll have to give me time, don't expect too much of me.

Pause.

I might seem very different. I might not be the me that you remember.

CLAIRE: Oh, you will, Gray. You just need to settle back in.

TOMMY: You don't know that, Claire.

CLAIRE: I don't care. You're coming home. That's all that matters to me. Oh, Gray, I missed you so much.

Beat.

Tell me you missed me, Gray.

Pause.

TOMMY: I missed you.

Beat.

Of course I did.

Pause.

CLAIRE: Tell me you love me.

Silence.

Gray?

TOMMY: Claire, I need you to do something for me.

CLAIRE: What is it, love?

TOMMY: Will you tell me about the last few months before I left?

Beat.

CLAIRE: No. It's all in the past now, I don't want to remember it.

TOMMY: Please, Claire.

CLAIRE: There's nothing to tell. You just left. That was it.

TOMMY: I know, but…just tell me about it, Claire, please.

CLAIRE: But why, Gray?

TOMMY: It might help me to remember.

Pause.

CLAIRE: Well, about six months before you…you'd had a heart scare, nothing too serious, just some chest pains, difficulty breathing, that kind of thing. You came home one day and said that you'd talked to Bob and the company could survive without you and you'd decided to take early retirement. You said that we could finally spend some proper time together…you'd been away a lot, what with one thing and another…training and business…so it would be nice. I was so happy.

TOMMY: Did…do you work?

CLAIRE: Yes, I still do. I work part-time as a receptionist for the local GP. Dr Gupta. He said to say he was looking forward to a round of golf when you get home, Gray.

TOMMY: I played golf?

CLAIRE: Oh yes, although you'd only just taken it up and we were having trouble getting membership of the golf club. They can be a bit snooty there. You used to say that they all had golf balls in their mouths instead of plums.

TOMMY: I was a bit of a joker, then?

CLAIRE: Oh, yes, always quick with the jokes, you were.

Pause.

TOMMY: How were things after I retired?

CLAIRE: It was wonderful. It was all I'd ever wanted, really. You were around the house more. You could spend some time on the garden and walking the dog and we could…

Beat.

TOMMY: Claire? What's wrong?

CLAIRE: It's…Gray…I had to have Whisky put down. Two years ago. Cancer.

TOMMY: Oh.

CLAIRE: I'm sorry.

Beat.

TOMMY: I'm sure you did what you thought was best.

CLAIRE: I did.

Beat.

She's buried in the garden. Bob helped.

TOMMY: Did he?

CLAIRE: Yes.

TOMMY: That's nice.

Pause.

CLAIRE: Anyway, we started to go out more than we had, y'know…evenings at the pub, the pictures…we even had a couple of dinner parties which was something we'd never done before. You cooked. You were always a much better cook than me.

TOMMY: Was I?

CLAIRE: Oh, yes. You said I could burn a salad.

Beat.

We were so happy, Gray. It was the best time of my life. Really. Just you and me in our little house. No stress, no worries.

Pause.

TOMMY: Can you tell me about the last day? The day I disappeared?

Beat.

CLAIRE: There's nothing to tell. I came home from work and you were gone.

TOMMY: Please, Claire.

Pause.

CLAIRE: You got up. You always got up earlier than me to walk Whisky. She'd always wake you by jumping on your bed and licking your face. I always kept my bedroom door closed so she couldn't do it to me.

Beat.

You woke me with a cup of tea when you got back and I got ready for work. It was one of my full days. We had breakfast as normal. Then I gave you a kiss and went to work and…

TOMMY: Did I say anything to you?

CLAIRE: What like?

TOMMY: I don't know. Just…anything different, anything strange.

CLAIRE: No.

Beat.

Well, I asked you about what you were going to do with your day and you said that you didn't know. Then you looked at me, deadly serious, and said that whatever you were going to do it was going to be extraordinary. That's the word you used. Extraordinary.

Beat.

I thought it was just one of your jokes, you were always trying to make me laugh. I didn't really understand your sense of humour.

Pause.

When I got home, your car was in the drive and I knew you'd be making dinner for us, as always. But when I got to the door, it was open…just a little bit but…I pushed it open all the way and called. You didn't answer. I thought you were probably in the garden. But then…Whisky had done her business everywhere and so I called again.

Beat.

I went into the kitchen and there, on the table, all laid out, neat and tidy…your keys, all in a row…and your bank books, credit cards, everything. I went upstairs but you weren't there. All your clothes were still in the wardrobe and…the clothes you'd been wearing that morning were laid on your bed. Like a dead body. Like you'd just melted out of them.

Beat.

I looked everywhere…but there was no note.

Pause.

That's the last time I saw you before today.

Pause.

And nobody could believe it. It was just so…out of character for you. You would never do anything like that, anything out of the ordinary. You're such a calm person…oh, you can be a bit moody sometimes but I never thought…for a second that you would…

Beat.

That's why we thought it must have been something suspicious. But nothing was missing…apart from what you'd done to the photos…you hadn't even taken any money out of your account. And nobody could think of any reason why anyone would want to hurt you. You've never done anything bad to anyone. The police said there was no law against going missing and you could do what liked. Nothing they could do, they said.

Silence.

Anyway, none of this matters now, because I've found you and here you are and we're back together and we can just put things behind us and go back to the way things were before.

Beat.

It'll be as though you never left.

Pause.

Gray?

TOMMY: I'm sorry, Claire.

CLAIRE: I know you are, love.

Pause.

I know you didn't mean to hurt me. I know you must have had your reasons. I don't mind.

Beat.

Just come home.

Silence.

TOMMY: Claire.

CLAIRE: Yes, Gray?

TOMMY: There's something I need to tell you.

CLAIRE: What is it?

Beat.

Oh, God, what have you done?

Pause.

What is it? You've done something awful, haven't you?

TOMMY gets up and walks away to the window.

It's alright, I've prepared myself for this. Whatever it is…just tell me…and we'll get through it together, I promise.

TOMMY: Don't make promises you can't keep.

Pause. He turns to her.

I never lost my memory.

Beat.

CLAIRE: I saw it in your eyes when you first saw me. I knew you knew me.

Beat.

Why have you been lying to me?

TOMMY: No, you don't understand.

CLAIRE: What don't I understand?

TOMMY: I never had amnesia. I made it up. I was just pretending.

Beat.

I know who I am.

CLAIRE: My Graham.

TOMMY: I know who I am. I always did. I know who I am. Who I was. Who I will be.

Beat.

There's only one thing I don't know.

CLAIRE: What's that?

TOMMY: Who you are.

Pause.

I've never seen you before in my life.

Pause.

CLAIRE: You're lying. Graham, I can tell you're lying.

TOMMY: My name isn't Graham, Claire. It's Tommy. Well, Thomas, actually.

Beat.

I've never met you before. I don't know who you are.

CLAIRE: Graham, stop it, you know it's me.

TOMMY: I can see that you're a very lonely woman, Claire. But trying to find a husband through the missing persons ads is just pitiful.

CLAIRE: How dare you say that to me? You walk out and leave me without so much as a goodbye…

TOMMY: Oh, I'm sure it must have been very hard for you…losing your husband in such a traumatic way. No explanation. I'm sure the life you had together was lovely. It sounds to me like the most boring fucking life anyone could imagine but I'm sure it must have worked for you.

CLAIRE: It worked for you too. We were happy.

TOMMY: I'm not him, Claire. You just want me to be.

CLAIRE: You are him, I mean, you. I know you are!

TOMMY: How do you know?

CLAIRE: Not that again! I just do!

TOMMY: Not good enough. How do you know?

CLAIRE: You look like him…like you.

TOMMY: You said yourself I look older. Don't you really mean different? As in totally different? And you weren't even sure it was me till you kissed me.

CLAIRE: No! No! You're Graham, my Graham. I know you are. Stop it! Stop this! It's not funny!

TOMMY: I'm not 'your' Graham, Claire. I understand that you might want to convince yourself that I am. Ideal for you – pick up some amnesiac, convince him he's your long lost husband, take him home, tell him you had a wonderful life – have a wonderful life all over again. Well, I'm sorry but not with me.

CLAIRE: Graham…

TOMMY: But, you know, even though I'm not him, I feel from what you've told me as if I know him. I even feel as if I could speak for him and I'm sure if he were here now, he'd say:

Pause. CLAIRE looks at him.

What are you doing here, Claire? Why are you still waiting for me?

Pause.

CLAIRE: He wouldn't say that.

TOMMY: Wouldn't he? Was it really so wonderful? Did he really make you so happy that it's worth spending five years of your life just hoping he'll come back? Can you afford to waste those years at your age? And what makes you think that he wants to come back?

Beat.

What makes you think that he wants to be found?

Pause.

CLAIRE: You bastard.

TOMMY: I hate tuna, Claire, it can't be me.

CLAIRE: This is just like you.

TOMMY: You don't know me.

CLAIRE: Oh, shut up, just shut up! I'm not stupid. I can see what you're doing. You couldn't just hurt me by leaving. No, that would be too easy for you. You couldn't just tell me the truth and leave me with some dignity. You've got to go through this whole pantomime just so you can enjoy hurting me another way.

TOMMY: I'm not trying to hurt you, Claire. I'm trying to help you.

CLAIRE: Then help me.

Beat.

You bastard.

TOMMY: Graham was a bastard. Tommy isn't.

CLAIRE: You are Graham.

TOMMY: God, don't you understand? It doesn't matter if I am or not! Graham, whoever he was, is long gone. He's five years gone, Claire, and he isn't coming back. Put him behind you. Move on. Throw out his clothes, sell his car, sell the house. Get together with Bob – it's clearly on the cards, he's alone, you're alone. But whatever you do, start living. Live each day like it's your last.

CLAIRE: Is that what you do?

Pause.

Why, Gray? What did I do?

TOMMY: Nothing.

Beat.

We've never met, Claire.

Long silence.

CLAIRE: You're right.

TOMMY: I know.

CLAIRE: You aren't him.

TOMMY: No.

CLAIRE: He would never treat me this way. He loves me. He wouldn't put me through this. He called me his angel. His angel. He wouldn't hurt me like this. You aren't him.

Pause.

CLAIRE: Let me see your hands.

TOMMY: Why?

CLAIRE: Let me see them.

TOMMY holds out his hands. She takes hold of them and studies them.

There, see!

TOMMY: What?

CLAIRE: Gray has a scar there, just by his thumb. His wrench slipped. It was very deep. Twelve stitches.

She shows him his hand.

See?

Pause.

TOMMY: Claire, I…

CLAIRE: I'm so sorry. I feel like such a fool. I should have thought. I should have remembered. I can't believe I didn't think of it. I'm so stupid.

Beat.

Thomas, I'm so sorry.

Beat.

TOMMY: That's…

CLAIRE: I hope this hasn't upset you too much.

Beat.

TOMMY: No, I…no.

CLAIRE gets up and goes to the door.

CLAIRE: Jean! Can you come in?

JEAN enters.

JEAN: Yes, Claire?

CLAIRE: Jean, I'm so sorry. There really has been the most terrible mistake.

JEAN: Oh?

CLAIRE: This man isn't my Graham.

JEAN: What?

CLAIRE: He isn't. I'm sure.

JEAN: But you said…

CLAIRE: Yes, I know and I can't believe I've been so stupid but, as I was just telling Tommy, Graham had a scar on his right palm.

JEAN: A scar?

CLAIRE: Yes, shaped like a heart, very distinctive. I should have remembered it earlier but it completely slipped my mind. Look.

CLAIRE takes TOMMY's hand and they all look at his palm.

You can see that Tommy hasn't got one.

Beat.

See?

JEAN: Yes, I see.

Pause.

I don't know what to say.

CLAIRE: It's my fault entirely.

JEAN: No, it's…

Beat.

Claire, are you sure?

CLAIRE: Of course I'm sure.

JEAN: Of course you are.

CLAIRE: He looks very like him, obviously, or I wouldn't have thought it was him in the first place but no, Graham was…Graham was…shorter.

Beat.

JEAN: Graham? I'm sorry, Tommy, er…did anything…do you remember anything? From what's been said today?

TOMMY shakes his head.

JEAN: Nothing at all?

Beat.

TOMMY: I'm in the dark.

Beat.

CLAIRE: It doesn't matter what he remembers. He isn't my Graham.

Beat.

JEAN: Claire, I'm sorry but…the scar notwithstanding …you were absolutely sure before I left that he was Graham…how can you be so certain that he isn't now?

CLAIRE: Because the last thing Gray said to me was that he was going to do something extraordinary.

Beat. She looks at TOMMY.

Does that look extraordinary to you?

Pause.

JEAN: Well, if you're sure then there's nothing I can say. Claire, I really am so very sorry about…I hope this hasn't been too distressing for you.

CLAIRE: No, it's fine.

JEAN: Sorry to get your hopes up.

CLAIRE: It was my fault.

Pause.

JEAN: What will you do now?

CLAIRE: What do you mean?

JEAN: Well, it's…it's been five years. Maybe it's time to…

CLAIRE: No.

Beat.

My Graham is out there somewhere. He's my life. He wouldn't want me to give up and I'm not going to. When he's ready to come home, I'll be waiting for him.

JEAN: But five years…

CLAIRE: It could be five years or fifty. I don't care. It's always been me for him and him for me and that's the way we like it. I just have to wait. He'll come back.

JEAN: What if he doesn't?

CLAIRE: He will. I know it.

Pause.

Well, I've just got time to get the next train, quite a journey back. Jean, thank you so much for all your help and I'm so sorry to have put you to all this trouble.

JEAN: Oh, not at all, it was a pleasure. I'm just sorry…

CLAIRE: Yes, and good luck with everything. I hope you manage to work things out with your husband. It doesn't matter how much we change, marriage is always worth fighting for, you know.

JEAN: I'm sure you're right.

CLAIRE: I know I am.

CLAIRE turns to TOMMY and holds out her hand.

Goodbye Thomas.

TOMMY: Goodbye.

They shake hands.

CLAIRE: Good luck.

TOMMY: Thank you.

JEAN: I'll…

CLAIRE: No, thank you. I'll see myself out.

CLAIRE leaves. Silence. TOMMY picks up his bag and starts to leave.

TOMMY: Well, I'll…

JEAN: What did you say to her?

TOMMY: Nothing.

JEAN: Don't give me that!

TOMMY: I didn't say anything to her!

JEAN: I don't believe you. Ten minutes ago, I walked out of this room and it was totally obvious you were going to go home with her. She was certain you were Graham and you believed her too. I walk back in to discover that she's 'remembered' a scar, which you don't have! It's bullshit! What did you say to her to make her change her mind?

TOMMY: I didn't…

JEAN: Graham!

TOMMY: No! She…we were just talking about me going home with her when she noticed my hand.

Beat.

That's it. That's what happened.

JEAN: You're lying.

TOMMY: You know, I've just had about enough of you calling me a liar. If anyone's a liar here, Jean, it's you.

Pause.

JEAN: I know what you're doing, y'know.

TOMMY: Oh, you do? Well, please enlighten me.

JEAN: You hated yourself, didn't you? You hated who you were and everything you'd done with your life. So you walked away. But you didn't actually have the guts to change. It takes real strength to become somebody new and you were just too scared. Too weak to go through with it. Better to be nobody than risk getting it wrong again. It's easier to be nothing. At least that way you don't despise yourself.

Beat.

Tell me I'm wrong.

Pause.

You can't, can you?

TOMMY: You talk about this with great authority, Jean.

JEAN: You're a coward.

TOMMY: Takes one to know one.

Pause.

JEAN: It sounded like a nice life. She's a nice woman. It's not as if there was anything really wrong, so why walk away? I don't understand it.

TOMMY: That's a nice suit.

Pause.

JEAN: Thank you.

TOMMY: It fits you well. It's a nice cut, nice cloth. You look good in it. It suits you.

Beat.

JEAN: Thank you. What…

TOMMY: I had a suit once. Grey. Business suit. Single breasted. Always wore it with a starched shirt and a plain tie.

Beat.

And I hated it. Absolutely hated it. It never really suited me. The collar cut into my neck. I couldn't breath when I was wearing it. You know what kind of suit I always wanted?

Beat.

A zoot suit. Bright pinstripes. Double breasted, with a waistcoat with a watch chain and wide braces and turn-ups. Broad brimmed hat. Spats with two-tone shoes.

Pause.

JEAN: That sounds like a nice suit.

TOMMY: It sounds better than nice, Jean.

Beat.

It sounds extraordinary.

Silence.

JEAN: Tommy, I'm so sorry.

TOMMY: Don't be.

Pause.

Like Claire said, it's not your fault. You did what you thought was best. You were trying to do a good turn. Couldn't be helped.

Beat.

I'm very grateful to you.

Pause.

Well, I'd…better get selling some of these Issues or I'll be hungry tonight.

JEAN reaches for her bag.

JEAN: Can I give you…

TOMMY: No.

JEAN: Please, it's no trouble.

TOMMY: No.

>*Beat.*

>Thank you.

>*Pause.*

>It was nice seeing you again.

JEAN: And you.

TOMMY: Maybe in another year we can do it again.

JEAN: That would be nice.

TOMMY: You won't find me though.

>*Beat.*

JEAN: No. Probably not.

>*Pause.*

TOMMY: Can you take my name off the Missing list? Can you do that?

>*Beat.*

JEAN: Of course.

TOMMY: Thank you.

>*Pause. He picks up his bag.*

>Well…goodbye.

JEAN: Goodbye.

>*TOMMY holds out his hand for JEAN to shake. She hugs him and kisses his cheek.*

>Good luck.

TOMMY: And to you.

TOMMY turns to leave. JEAN's voice stops him in the doorway.

JEAN: Tommy…

TOMMY: Yes?

Pause.

JEAN: It would be very sad.

TOMMY: What would?

JEAN: If we spent the rest of our lives being nobody just to avoid being somebody.

Pause.

TOMMY: Maybe you're right.

They look at each other.

He goes, closing the door behind him.

The noise of the children playing grows louder.

JEAN sits alone. After a few moments she gets up, takes off her jacket and puts it and her briefcase full of files into a box of jumble.

She picks up her overcoat and handbag.

She looks up at her graffiti. She smiles.

She exits, leaving the door open. The sound of the children continues.

End of Play.